The Usborne Creative Writing Book

With writing by

Write your
name here.

Contents

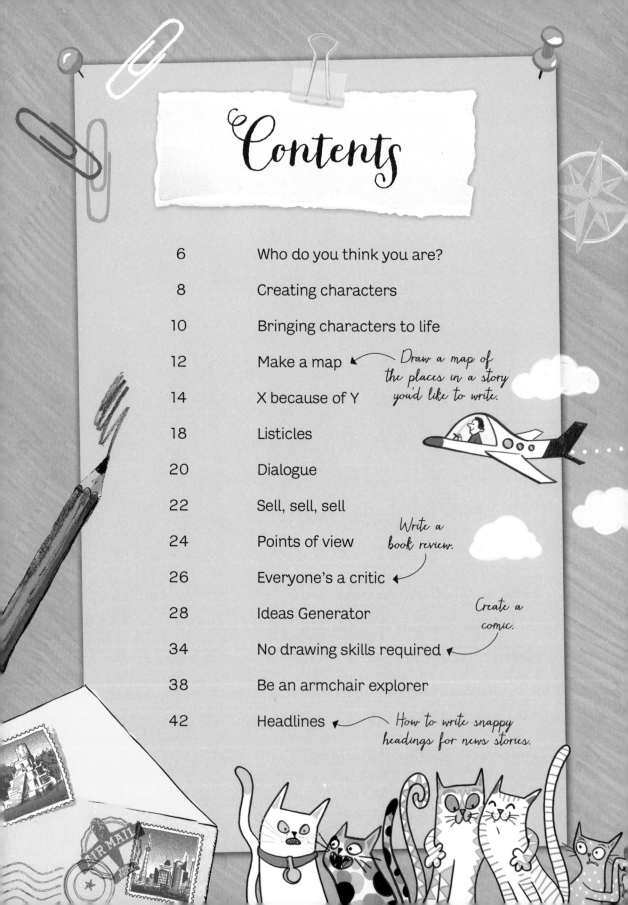

Draw a map of the places in a story you'd like to write.

Write a book review.

Create a comic.

How to write snappy headings for news stories.

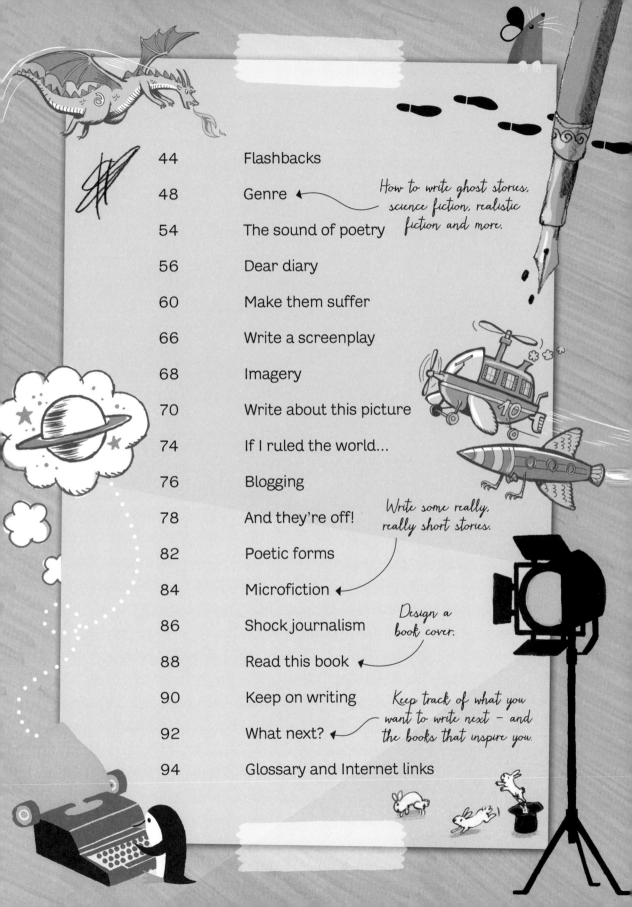

Who do you think you are?

A good place to start your writing is with a subject close to your heart — you.

Name: Lizbeth

Age: 9

Height:

Hair:

Eyes:

Three words that describe me:

The most unusual thing about me:

I live in

I live with

My friends are

What I like best about them is

Three things that make me **laugh**:

Three things that make me *cry*:

Three things that make me angry:

My *hobbies* are

I am especially good at

I'd like to learn to

My greatest **strength** is

My greatest weakness is

I'm most *afraid* of

The last book I read was

What I enjoyed most about it was

POST CARD

If I could be invisible for a day, I would

If I could have
three wishes
they would be

One day, my *ambition* is to

Creating characters

Where do characters come from? Sometimes, they pop into your mind fully formed. If not, there are lots of tricks you can use to help you create believable, interesting characters.

People you know

Think about people you know — their appearance, their hopes, their bad habits.

If you take a personality trait here and a burning desire there from lots of different people, you can create a brand new character.

Listen

Keep your ears open for snippets of conversation. Something you overhear might give you a starting point for a character.

For every strength...

Think of a list of strengths, then come up with an equal number of weaknesses.

You could make the weaknesses reflect the strengths. For example, a character who has passionate beliefs might also have a very short temper.

Or a very hard-working, successful character might not be good at relaxing or having fun.

Unlikely pairings

Try creating characters by mixing and matching things that don't normally go together. For example...

Fairy + police officer

Rabbit + fierce

Baby + astronaut

Insect + princess

Create a character by filling in the questionnaire on the next page.

CHARACTER QUESTIONNAIRE

Name:

Age:

Appearance:

Personality:

Goal in life:

STRENGTHS:

WEAKNESSES:

Greatest problem:

FRIENDS:

KNOWN ENEMIES:

Bringing characters to life

In real life, people's words and actions tell you something about them. In a similar way, you can give readers an idea about the personality of the characters you write about through what they say and do. This is called characterization.

Flesh them out

You can reveal your character through...

Speech

The way people speak, as well as what they talk about, says a lot about them. For example, a shy person might talk quietly, and a nervous person could speak quickly.

Objects

Personal property of...

A character's possessions can be revealing. You could show that a person is eccentric by the unusual things in his or her bag or pockets, for example.

Appearance

How do your character's clothes reflect his or her personality?

Someone who's a stickler for rules might wear formal clothes, while a show-off might have an elaborate hairstyle.

Relationships

How does your character interact with others? Is she kind? Does he start fights? Do other people warm to her or find her annoying?

Drip-feed information

You don't need to tell your reader everything about a character all at once. You can reveal things bit by bit, only giving away what's relevant to the story as it unfolds.

Pick a character

Use this page to write about a typical day in the life of a real or fictional character.

Include details about your character's appearance, possessions, speech patterns and relationships with others to help you bring her, him or it to life.

Someone you know

Someone famous

Someone from history

The character you created on page 9

Make a map

Use these pages to draw a map of the setting for a story you'd like to write. Include lots of interesting places for your characters to explore. It could be a fantastical land or an ordinary town or village.

Haunted house

Spaceship launchpad

Having a strong sense of the setting of a story before you start writing can help you write vividly. It can also prevent confusion about your characters' comings and goings.

X because of Y

Writing a step-by-step plan of what happens in each part of your story can really help to give it a satisfying structure to drive the action forward.

Causation

In the best stories, each new event happens *because* of what's gone before. Nothing is random.

For example,

A detective is called to a house **because** someone has found the body of an old lady. There's been a murder.

Because she finds an unusual animal hair at the scene, the detective suspects the victim's lodger, who breeds rare animals.

Because she picks up this hair, she sneezes — she's allergic to animals. The lodger gives her a tissue and she sees blood on his hand...

...and so on.

Motivation

One way to make your story flow is to give your characters solid motives for their actions — and make sure those actions have consequences that matter.

What makes your characters do what they do?

Revenge

Jealousy

Fear

Feeling betrayed by someone

A DESIRE FOR FAME

Greed

Love

From beginning to end

Breaking down a story plan into sections can help you plot each step of the journey through your story.

Beginning
Here the main character is introduced and the scene is set.

Build-up
Something happens that changes the hero's situation.

Climax
The main character confronts a big problem.

Resolution
The problem is resolved in some way.

End
The loose ends of your story are tied up and you show how things have changed for your character since the start.

A story outline

Plan a story below, thinking about character motivations, and how each event flows on to the next. Start your story on the next page.

Beginning
Who is your character?
Where does the story take place?

Build-up
What happens to get the story started?
What does your character do about it?

Climax
What problem does your character face?
How does it link to what's gone before?

Resolution
How does your character resolve the situation?
How does the resolution flow from the climax?

End
Think about how your character feels at the end. Is it a happy ending? Sad? A mix?

Write your
story title here.

The plan is not set in stone

If you have a new idea for your story while you're writing, you can always change your plan. Sometimes you only find out what your story is really about by writing it.

Doom   **Consequences**

Fear and flight   *Wisdom*

People change

Although your characters should be driven by strong motivations, they don't have to want the same thing all the way through.

Someone who's been through a lot might come to see things in a new light by the end of the story.

The end

Unfortunately   *Life-changing*   A choice   **FATAL ERROR**   "If only I'd never..."

Fate   *Achievement*   **RESPONSIBILITY**   Discovering   **GROWING**

Listicles

A listicle is an article written like a list. A list means you don't have to link one item to the next — which gives you a lot of freedom to pull random ideas and insights together.

Pick a number and a topic

Listicles often start with a number. Think about what you want your list to be about and make sure you can think of *that many* things to go on your list.

Some examples of headings

19 reasons why Star Wars is the best movie in history

9 tips for surviving at school

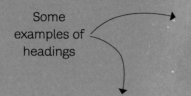

17 books that will make you wish you lived inside them

27 disgusting things you probably don't know about restaurants

12 facts about goats that will shock you

Topic ideas

- Books, movies or TV shows that you love or hate with a passion

- Facts that you almost can't believe are true

- Famous people who did really weird jobs when they were trying to make it big

- Your pets or hobbies

- The world's weirdest ice cream varieties

Write a listicle below. You could illustrate it too, or stick in pictures that you've printed out or cut out of magazines.

Write your headline here. (See page 42 for some tips on headline writing.)

Add pictures here.

Dialogue

When characters talk to each other in a story, it's called dialogue.

Showing dialogue

When you write dialogue, the words characters say should be shown inside speech marks. Here are some more tips to help you out:

> The King raised his hand. "What's the meaning of this intrusion?" he demanded.
>
> "Please, Your Majesty," said Leila, "my friends and I are in trouble."

The first word of a spoken sentence begins with a capital letter.

Start a new line for each new speaker, using commas to separate the speech from the rest of the sentence.

If you end a sentence with speech, the punctuation goes inside the speech marks.

Use speech to...

Find out how to write dialogue in a screenplay on page 66 and in a comic strip on page 34.

...show a character's personality. For example, a rude person might interrupt a lot.

...convey someone's mood. If nervous or upset, a character's speech might become broken-up and stammering.

...show relationships between characters. Are they friends sharing a joke or enemies trading insults?

...introduce conflict. Arguments can be more fun to read than everyone saying, "I agree," all the time.

...reveal information. For example, a character could confess to a murder.

...make action more dramatic. Instead of describing a scary thing appearing, a character could shout, "Look out!"

Rrrr?

Did you hear?

What?

Mittens had to go to the VET!

Meow!

Prr!

Does this mouse smell ok to you?

Look out! Bulldog!

20

Use this page to write a dramatic conversation between two characters.

"

Who are your characters? Are they friends, strangers or rivals?

Maybe one of the characters just wants to tell the others a joke.

Does anything happen to interrupt the dialogue? Does someone else come along?

"

Character suggestions

A brother and sister

A superhero and supervillain

Cats in a backyard

Fighter pilots in two different planes

Sell, sell, sell

To persuade someone that a product is worth buying, you have to think your way into the mind of the potential buyer. Writing a good advertisement is halfway between being a psychologist and a writer.

Advertisements appeal to customers using a combination of...

Logic

What is the product used for? If it's not the only product of its kind, why is this brand better than all the others?

Word ideas

Desire

What do the buyers want out of life? How can you persuade them that this product can provide what they crave?

Fear

Is the potential customer afraid of being alone? Of being a failure? Of being ugly? How might buying your product take away those fears?

Soft
Durable
Sparkling
Improve
Energy
TRANSFORM
Taste
Safety
Discover
Health
Dreamer
Perfect
Crunch
Speed
Perform
Freedom

Laughter

Can you make your audience laugh? Laughter can make people more receptive to the message you're trying to get across.

Name:

Slogan:

Name:

Slogan:

Slogan:

Name:

Name:

Slogan:

Points of view

Stories are always seen through the eyes of a narrator — the person who is telling the story. Who is your narrator? A character involved in the story? Or an outsider, looking in?

First person — 'I' or 'we'

This is when your narrator is a character within the story. The reader is watching the action through the main character's eyes.

Continue the story below, which is written in the first person. Think about what the narrator felt and thought, coming face-to-face with a tiger.

My heart was pounding. I looked back, and could see the
tiger's eyes flashing at me...

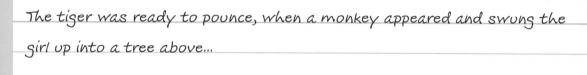

Third person — 'he', 'she' or 'they'

If your story is being told by a narrator outside the
story, this is called the third person. It's a useful way
of showing the action from more than one angle.

Continue the story in the third person.

The tiger was ready to pounce, when a monkey appeared and swung the

girl up into a tree above...

You can also concentrate on the thoughts
and actions of just one character while
writing in the third person.

Continue the story below, telling the
story in the third person, but from
the tiger's viewpoint.

The tiger licked his lips. The girl looked delicious, he thought...

Second person — 'you'

This point of view is rarely used. Imagine your
reader IS the main character in the story.
This draws your reader into the action.

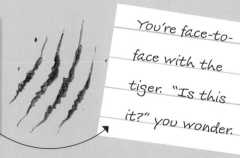

*You're face-to-
face with the
tiger. "Is this
it?" you wonder.*

25

Everyone's a critic

Critics use the power of words to convince us to watch shows, read books or eat in restaurants — or not to. How do they do it? Here are some tips, and useful words, for writing persuasive book reviews.

Read me NOW!

Start your review with a must-read headline followed by a bold opening sentence.

What was it about the book that really made it worth reading?

No spoilers...

Describe what the book is about without explaining the entire plot.

You might share one or two dramatic high points, but avoid giving too much away. Leave readers wanting to read the book to find out more.

Spectacular
Nail-biting
Gripping
Brilliant

Devastating
HEARTWARMING
Traumatic
Unexpected

How does it make you feel?

Describe how you feel about the book and why. Did you find it scary and disturbing or funny and sweet? Did that feeling linger after you had finished reading it?

Write a review of a book you love or hate on this page.

Give your review a headline.

Your verdict

End your review by summing up your opinion. Sometimes it's more effective not to do this with an 'I' sentence. Which of these sounds more persuasive to you?

I really liked this book and I think you should read it.

This is a dazzling, heart-stopping story that you won't be able to put down.

You might like to give your book a star rating too.

Ideas Generator

Every story starts with an idea. Sometimes all you need is a word or an image to get started. Create your own Ideas Generator following the instructions below.

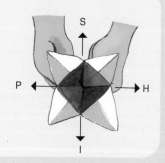

Instructions

① Cut along the dotted lines on the page opposite.

② Lay the square with the blank side up.

③ Fold each corner into the middle.

④ It will look like this. Now turn it over.

⑤ Fold each corner into the middle again.

⑥ It will look like this.

⑦ Fold in half so it looks like this.

⑧ Fold in half again to make a crease.

⑨ Unfold so the square flaps lie along the bottom.

⑩ Slide your thumbs and fingers under each square flap and pinch.

How to play

Ⓐ Once you've made your Ideas Generator, try pinching and pulling with your fingers to open and close it.

Ⓑ Pick a setting from the top, such as 'ship'. Spell out the word, and open and close the Generator each time you *say* a letter.

S
P ← → H
I

Ⓒ Stop when you say the last letter. Pick a character from inside and read out its number. Open and close the Generator that number of times.

1
4 ← → 2
3

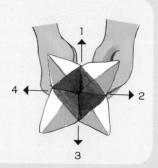

Ⓓ Then pick another character. Lift the flap and read out the event or situation underneath.

28

When you've picked a setting, characters and event, you can plan your story on the next page.

This side has been left blank so you can make a new Ideas Generator using your own ideas.

Fill the green triangles with characters.

Fill the yellow triangles with settings.

Fill the blue triangles with events.

Once you've filled in all the triangles, follow steps 3–10 in the instructions. This time start with the printed pictures facing up.

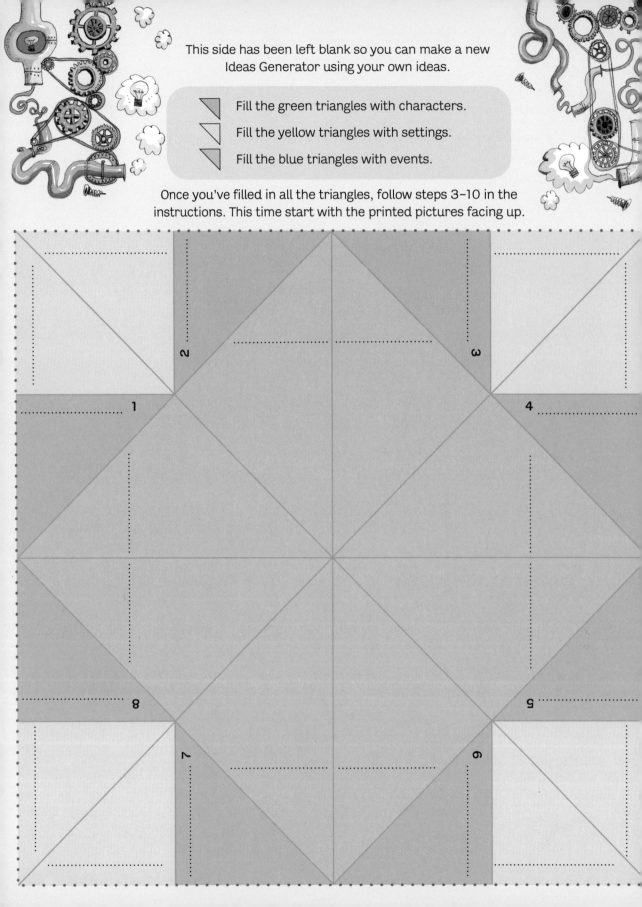

Use the ideas you've generated to plan your story below.

Character 1
Who is your main character? Describe his or her weaknesses and strengths.

Character 2
Is your secondary character a friend or an enemy?

Setting
What does your setting look, sound or feel like?

Beginning
Use the event you picked to get your story started. Does it create challenges for your characters?

What next?
How do your characters deal with the challenge? Do they work together or against each other to reach a solution?

In the end
Does your story have a happy or a sad ending? Where do your characters end up?

Now use the next two pages to write your story.

Find more **Ideas Generators** at the Usborne Quicklinks website – go to **www.usborne.com/quicklinks** and type the keywords '**creative writing**'.

31

Write your story
title here. →

The end

No drawing skills required

One way to tell a story is in a comic strip.

Comics use speech bubbles, like this, for dialogue.

Thoughts go in cloud-shaped bubbles like this.

You don't need amazing drawing skills. To create a character, just add accessories to a stick figure.

Here are a few poses and expressions to show different actions and moods.

Sound effects can come in handy, too.

Sploosh!

ZOOOM!

Oh, and the boxes in a comic are called panels.

Here's an example of how to tell a story in six panels.

Beginning

Build-up

Something happens
to kickstart the story.

Middle

Climax

This should be the tensest or most exciting moment.

Resolution

The main problem or tension is resolved here. In this case it no longer seems that the bear might eat the rabbit.

End

Turn over to make your own comic strip.

35

Plan your own comic story here, writing what will happen in each panel. There are some ideas at the bottom of the page to help you, or you could use the Ideas Generator on page 29.

Beginning

Build-up

Middle

Climax

Resolution

End

use the Ideas Generator on page 29.

Story ideas

A frog gets a job as a fashion model.

A teenager wakes up as the President of the United States.

You find a map that leads you to pirate treasure.

The Moon disappears and a detective with superpowers has to find out why.

Draw and write your comic strip in these blank panels.

Be an armchair explorer

How do you write about the thrills of spaceflight, or the sights of distant cities, if you're not an astronaut and you've never been to another country? The answer is simple: research.

You can make your story convincing by weaving facts into your fiction. Here are a few ways to discover those crucial details.

Visit a library

Libraries are great sources for books on all kinds of subjects.

They may also have old maps or atlases, newspaper archives or rare manuscripts.

Talk to your librarian, who will be able to help guide your search.

Talk to experts

Find people who have had interesting experiences. You'll find that many people are eager to share their stories.

If you ask the right questions, you can discover things that aren't written down anywhere.

Study the world around you

Take notes on what you see, hear, feel, taste and smell, how people dress, and how they talk.

These can all be used to add believable detail and richness to your writing.

Search the internet

You can find articles, news stories and videos and view satellite maps of distant countries and cities online — but you have to be cautious.

To find tips and advice about searching the internet safely, go to the Usborne Quicklinks website at **www.usborne.com/quicklinks** and type the keywords **'creative writing'**.

Plan a letter

Do some research about a place you've never visited. It could be a distant island, a busy city or one of Jupiter's moons. Write some notes below, then use the details to write a letter to a friend about an imaginary adventure, on the next page.

How do you get there? How do you travel once you're there?

What does the air smell like (if there's air)?

What do you eat there?

Place name:

Have any famous events ever happened there?

Who or what lives there?

Now write your letter on these pages.

It could describe a voyage of discovery, a gripping chase, a delicious meal — or any experience you think could happen in the place you've chosen.

Put the address of the place you're visiting here.

_____

_____

_____

_____

Dear _____

_____

_____

_____

_____

_____

_____

_____

_____

_____

_____

_____

_____

AIR MAIL

Place word ideas

Thick clouds
Salty air

Love from,

Torrential floods   *Rolling hills*   **Deadly fumes**   ANCIENT RUINS

Towering skyscrapers   SHINING GLASS   Quaint cottages   **Black ice** 41

HEADLINES

A good headline in a magazine or news article tells you what the article is about and makes you want to read on. Here are some tips for writing headlines that make a big impact with only a few words.

Headlines don't have to be full sentences.

Slang and abbreviations can help save you space.

Cut unnecessary words. You can go into detail in the article.

WOMAN ON MARS

~~Grandmother~~ **GRAN** ~~rescued~~ **SAVED BY SEA** ~~helicopter~~ **CHOPPER**

~~Furry~~ **MONSTER** ~~with big pink eyes~~ **SPOTTED IN MOUNTAINS**

Now try rewriting these sentences to turn them into snappy headlines.

A girl has been awarded a science prize for her new invention.	Some local children have come first in a talent competition.	A rare purple flower with an orange stem has been found in a park by the swings.

PLAYING WITH WORDS

These wordplay techniques can help to catch readers' attention.

Rhyme

Alliteration — repeating the same letter sound.

Puns — jokes using words that have more than one meaning.

The Herald

MOOSE ON LOOSE

The Daily Report

PRINCE PICKS PUP

Local 🛡 News

AQUARIUM GETS SEAL OF APPROVAL

Try writing headlines to go with these news stories and pictures.

Archaeologists in Mexico have discovered a hoard of treasure buried over 500 years ago.

Rovers took the championship after their star player, Scott Storrie, scored the winning goal against United.

Marco's Pizza has been named the country's very best restaurant after a public vote.

Flashbacks

You don't have to tell a story in chronological order. Using a flashback catapults your readers to a point earlier in the story. This allows you to show something in the past that has a direct effect on the events in the present.

Flashbacks often take the form of a memory. This could be triggered by an object, a taste, a sound or a smell that takes a character back in time.

> Tom took a bite out of the mango, and a memory of the day before they'd set sail flooded back.
>
> He'd been slumped on a sack of grain outside the Bajan Inn. It had made a convenient place for someone who couldn't afford to go inside to rest and watch the world go by.
>
> If only he had been inside he might not have met...

Desert island challenge

Plan a story set on a desert island using a flashback to explain how the main character got there.

First, create a timeline for your story.

Then, jot down the order in which you want to write about those events. The flashback could go somewhere in the middle.

1.

2.

3.

4.

5.

6.

Write your story title here.

Make it stand out

Make sure your flashback stands out from the parts of the story set in the present.

If your main story is written in the present tense, write the flashback in the past tense.

If your story is in the past tense, put your flashback further back in time, using words such as 'had' in the first few sentences: "It had been a long hot summer..."

Continue your story on the next page.

Washed up Marooned *Shadowy* **SNARLING** Jungle Parched

Natural spring   Campfire   Hunting

The end

Genre

Types of stories, such as ghost stories or thrillers, are known as genres. Each genre has its own conventions — typical themes, settings, plot structures and writing styles.

Here are some genres you could use in your stories.

Fantasy

- Characters include dragons, elves and brave warriors.
- The plot often includes a quest for a magical object or lots of big battles.

Ghost story

- Haunted house setting is common
- At least one character is a ghost.
- Plot is often about why the ghost is there.
- Can be scary or funny

Comedy

- Plot usually includes lots of misunderstandings.
- Characters can be funny without realizing it, or witty on purpose.
- Ending usually happy

Realistic fiction

- Settings are everyday, like your real life.
- Themes include families, relationships and feelings.
- Enemies could include rivals, bullies — or very annoying siblings.

Combining genres

A story can be in several genres at once. You might want to write a science fiction murder mystery, or a historical romance, for example.

Genre isn't a prison for your ideas, it's a jumping-off point.

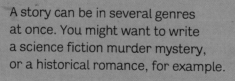

Horror

- Almost everyone dies
- Main character battles nearly-unstoppable villains.
- Villains include dolls that come to life, evil clowns, murderers and aliens.

Science fiction

- Settings include other planets, spaceships or alien invasions.
- Stories often answer a "what if...?" question.
- Can involve time travel.
- Characters could have futuristic gadgets.

Historical

- Set in the past
- Could include battles and other big events, but also daily life.
- Characters can be famous figures or made-up people from that time.

Thriller

- Plot has a lot of action.
- There's often a race against time.
- Main characters are often spies.
- People chase each other across rooftops a lot.

Romance

- Heroes are handsome, heroines are beautiful.
- Characters fall in love.
- A lot of things get in the way of them getting together, but the end is happy.

Detective

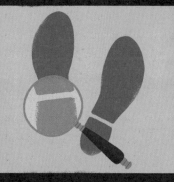

- Main character usually a detective (police, private detective, someone else investigating a crime)
- A crime is usually solved by the end of the story.

Pick a genre (or two) and turn the page to start your own story.

Use this page to plan your genre story.

Genre(s):	Main character:	Setting:

Beginning:

What happens to kickstart the story?

Build-up:

What adds to the tension? A ghost appears? A quest begins? The main character falls in love?

Middle:

What problems does the main character face? Think about the types of enemies, situations and events that fit your genre.

Climax:

This is the dramatic high point. Your main character faces his or her greatest challenge.

End:

Is the ending happy? Do all the problems get solved? Is there an action-packed final scene? Does anyone die?

Now write your story on the next three pages.

Write your title here.

Exaggeration

To make your story funny, you could try exaggerating the genre's conventions.

For example, in a romance story, you could make the hero so handsome people fall over when he turns up. Or in a thriller, you could have an incredibly brave main character who does ludicrously risky things.

Continue your story on the next page.

Parachute   DIVORCE   Clues   Swashbuckling

Eerie   Cursed mirror   SPACE STATION

The end

Revolutionaries   Undercover agent

CANNONS   Alien abduction   Passion

The sound of poetry

When you're writing poems, it helps to think about how they will sound when spoken aloud. Imagine that they are songs in which the words make their own music.

Rhyme

You can use rhyme — words that end with the same sound — to tie lines together. Write a rhyming poem here. You could use the rhymes provided, or come up with your own.

These letters show a pattern of rhyming lines known as a rhyme scheme.

——————————————— seek   a

——————————————— vile   b

——————————————— peak   a

——————————————— file   b

——————————————— bell   c

——————————————— free   d

——————————————— swell   c

——————————————— three   d

——————————————— grunt   e

——————————————— chafe   f

——————————————— blunt   e

——————————————— safe   f

——————————————— admire   g

——————————————— retire   g

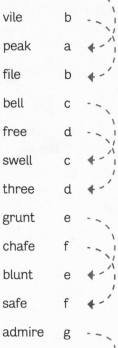

This particular pattern of rhymes was made famous by William Shakespeare. He used it in a long series of 14-line poems called *sonnets*.

Alliteration and assonance

Try using several words together that start with the same sound. This is called *alliteration* when you use consonants, and *assonance* when you use vowel sounds.

Complete the lines below using alliteration or assonance.

The rickety raft went riding through rollicking rapids.

Every elephant

On dark days

Why bees buzz

Some words — like *buzz*, *moo* and *squelch* — sound like the thing they describe. This is called *onomatopoeia* (sounds like "on-oh-mah-toe-PEA-ah"). These words can make people feel they're actually hearing the scene you're describing.

Add some more onomatopoeic words to the list below.

zoom zap! **Splash**

SNIP murmur meow

Write your own poem...

...using alliteration, assonance, rhyme and onomotopoeia.

scritch scratch

Give your
poem a title.

You could try this
rhyme scheme.

a

a

b

b

c

c

55

Dear diary

Try making a comic strip about yourself. It could focus on something that happened an hour ago, or the story of your whole life so far.

Here's a sample comic showing some techniques you could use in your strip.

Show time passing between panels by adding captions like this.

You could use exaggeration.

Captions can show a change of location....

...or to allow a character to talk directly to the reader.

Labels with arrows can help to make it clear what's happening.

Plan your comic

On the next page, you'll have 12 panels to draw and write your comic.
Use this page to plan what you'd like to put in each panel.

1.

2.

3.

4.

5.

6.

7.

8.

9.

10.

11.

12.

You could include conversations you've had.

And arguments too!

You could write about your feelings.

Draw your comic strip diary in these 12 panels.

Make them suffer

When you're writing a story, force your characters to face large obstacles. This will make your writing more gripping.

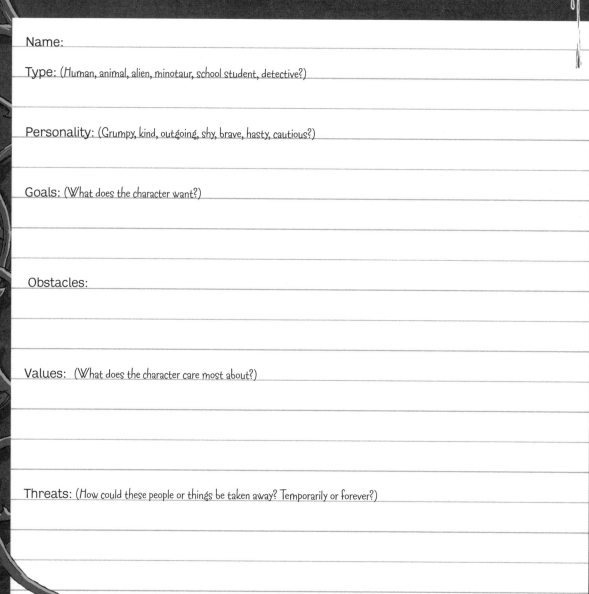

In the spaces below, create a character, and plan how to make his or her life an absolute misery.

Name:

Type: (Human, animal, alien, minotaur, school student, detective?)

Personality: (Grumpy, kind, outgoing, shy, brave, hasty, cautious?)

Goals: (What does the character want?)

Obstacles:

Values: (What does the character care most about?)

Threats: (How could these people or things be taken away? Temporarily or forever?)

Plan your story

Below, plan a story featuring the character you've just created,
full of bad luck, cruelty, accidents and terrible decisions.

One day, your character is (Doing what? Where?)

Your character reacts by

Then, something else goes horribly wrong.

Your character tries to solve the problem by

But, to add insult to injury (Add another misfortune.)

In the end (Are the things your character lost restored? Or does it all end badly?)

Begin your story on the next page.

> Death is fine,
> but please don't
> embarrass me.

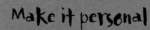

Make it personal

Fit the suffering to your character's personality.

For example, someone who cares what other people think will suffer if he or she is publicly humiliated. You don't have to kill a character's friends and family to create suffering.

Measles Broken promise

Hole in the ground

Write your story
title here.

Wrongful arrest Alone Howl Exam failure

Squashed hamster

GRIEF

Rays of hope

Give your character some moments of happiness, or at least hope, to keep the story varied.

You could make it seem as though everything might be ok again, before plunging the character back into difficulty, danger and pain.

One final misfortune

Even if you're going to give the story a happy ending, try to include a moment near the end when everything seems truly lost. Make readers believe your character cannot get out of this.

Nothing but rubble

The end

Write a screenplay

Screenplays are scripts for movies. They set out the story, the characters and the dialogue for the director and actors to use when shooting a movie.

The beginning of a story, as it might look in a book:

"How much further?" groaned Anna.
"Can't imagine we'll be home until midnight," replied Rob, switching on the car radio to keep himself awake. The announcer sounded worried. "Police are advising everyone to get home as soon as possible. A dangerous criminal is on the loose."

This is how the same scene could look as a screenplay. Screenwriters have a particular way of setting things out.

A new scene starts when the setting or time changes. The setting goes under the scene number.

```
                    SCENE 1
                CAR - AT NIGHT


      ANNA, a young woman, and her boyfriend
          ROB drive home. They look tired.


                     ANNA
                How much further?


                     ROB
                  (to Anna)
      Can't imagine we'll be home until midnight.


              He switches on the radio.


               RADIO ANNOUNCER
                  (worried)
          Police are advising everyone to get
          home as soon as possible. A dangerous
               criminal is on the loose.
```

New characters are introduced at the start of a scene.

This shows who the character is talking to, if it's not clear already.

Notes like this tell the actors how to say their lines.

Dialogue is set out like this.

'Action lines' tell the actors what to do. They're written in the present tense.

Continue writing the scene from the previous page,
or try writing a scene for your own movie.

What kind of movie is it? Horror? Comedy? Action?

Script tips

You could suggest music for the soundtrack, and include sound effects in your script.

Your characters don't have to speak in complete sentences. People often tail off mid-sentence.

Try writing an action sequence: a section of the script with lots of action and not much dialogue.

Imagery

Imagery is a way of describing things that creates pictures in the reader's imagination. Imagery helps bring ideas and emotions to life.

Two common forms of imagery are called similes and metaphors.

Similes

A simile compares one thing to something else. The words 'as' and 'like' are often used:

- He was always as quiet *as* a mouse.

Shh...

- She was wrinkled and brown, *like* a grape left out in the sun.

Try your hand at some similes.

Her eyes were like

The sand was dry and white like

The old woman was as angry as

Metaphors

When you use metaphor you describe something as if it were something else — often something you wouldn't normally associate with that thing:

- Life is a bowl of cherries.

- My legs turned to jelly.

- Her hair is seaweed, wet and wild, slippery, salt-scented.

Try writing your own metaphors below.

Let your imagery run wild!

Write a poem or a descriptive passage about someone you know, using metaphors and similes. Does that person resemble a flower or a tree, perhaps? Does the way he or she moves remind you of a wild animal? Does his or her voice sound like a particular musical instrument?

Sensory imagery

Remember: imagery need not be visual. Taste, touch, sound and smell are all important too.

Imagery ideas

His opinions leave a sour taste.

Her smile is as sweet as honey.

He is as cold as a glacier.

His hair is like straw.

Her heart is a nest of spiders.

HER VOICE IS AS LOUD AS A FOGHORN.

He has the stench of failure about him.

69

Write about this picture

A picture can make your mind wander to interesting places. Write a story, an article, a poem — or anything you like — about the picture opposite.

Some ideas

Make up a story, using one of the people or animals as the main character.

Write about how the picture makes you feel.

Describe an event in your life that this image brings to mind.

Write an interview with one of the characters in the picture.

Imagine a conversation between two of the characters, and write it as a screenplay.

Continue on the next two pages.

Precisely the right word

When you're describing a scene or an emotion, think carefully about the words you choose.

For example, is the emotion you want to convey anger? Is it rage? Or is it something more gentle, like mild irritation?

You could try saying a few different words out loud (or in your head) to see what sounds right.

Illusion   Down   Big top   Gasp

Excitement   Delight   Roar

The end

High wire   Fortune teller

Stampede   *Shock*   Lion tamer

If I ruled the world...

Imagine you are standing for election to become President of the world. What changes would you introduce and how would you persuade people to vote for you?

Your campaign poster

First, design a poster showing voters what you stand for. You could include a striking logo or a memorable slogan that sums up your campaign.

Your big speech

Next, write an awe-inspiring speech to persuade people to vote for you. Here are some tips:

Write the way you speak. Read your speech aloud as you go. If anything sounds unnatural, rewrite it.

Start with a bold opening line and repeat it with variations to make it stick.
"I swear to you... I swear to you now that this planet will not die."

Set out a question or problem, then outline how you plan to solve it.
"Not enough time to play? Here's how I will change all that..."

Use what's known as 'the rule of three' to make your audience take notice.
"I promise to defend truth, justice and the Martian way."

Conclude your speech with a snappy summary that appeals directly to your audience.
"So, vote for me and no child will ever go hungry again."

Policy ideas   Set up the first colony on Mars   Save the environment   Ban the bomb   Enough food for everyone   Eradicate racism

Write your speech here. →

Slogan Make peace not war! Deeds not together! Everyone together! In it to win it! Yes we can!

Blogging

A blog is an online journal. You don't have to write about your daily life — just pick a topic that fascinates you. Blogs often have titles that sum up what they're about.

Setting up a blog

All you need to do to start a blog is set up an account at a blogging platform. Most of them are free, and there are plenty of options.

Go to **www.usborne.com/quicklinks** and type the keywords **'creative writing'** to find technical tips about starting a blog.

If you are under 13, you will need a parent or teacher to set up an account and supervise the blog.

Pick a focus

Try to stick to a single theme. This gives your blog a strong identity, and helps you come up with ideas.

Blog theme ideas

- New books you've read
- Weird animals
- Meals you've eaten
- A sport you're obsessed with
- Jokes you've heard
- Your poetry
- Comic book characters you love
- What you want to do when you're an adult
- Fashion

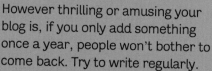

Keep up the pace

However thrilling or amusing your blog is, if you only add something once a year, people won't bother to come back. Try to write regularly.

If in doubt, be positive

Angry rants online can be fun to read, but it's hard to write them without sounding bitter and attracting negative attention.

Keeping a positive tone to your blog is often the best way to get people to engage with it nicely.

Leave comments

If you read other people's blogs and leave nice comments, people are more likely to read your blog in return.

What would you like to write a blog about? Think about the general theme, then write a first post below. (Any time you put something up on your blog, it's known as a post.)

My blog theme is

My blog is called

My first blog post will be about

The title for my first post is

Write your post on this page. You could post it later. Be very careful not to share any personal information online.

Give your post a title.

And they're off!

Imagine you're a sports commentator, giving a live report on a dramatic race. It could be a competition between real athletes, or a race between fantastical characters.

Muscular writing

Sports reports often use what's known as a 'muscular' style, using strong verbs (action words) and short, punchy sentences. So, instead of this:

> *"She **leaves** the starting blocks and **runs very fast** to the finish."*

Write something like this:

> *"She **springs** from the starting blocks and **sprints** to the finish. "*

Using the present tense adds excitement, as though the race is immediately in front of you.

Try rewriting this in a more muscular style.

> *"The pistol went off and the race began. The racers ran quickly, jumped over the first hurdle then climbed up the cargo net."*

_____

_____

_____

_____

_____

Set the scene

Make your readers feel as though they are watching with you. Describe how the crowd reacts to events, and the atmosphere, sights, sounds and smells surrounding the race.

But remember to return to the action.

Vary the pace

Try slowing down the action at a particularly tense moment. Describe every tiny detail – a bead of sweat on a racer's brow, the thud of feet on the race track or the grind of gears changing.

Then, speed things up with a sudden dramatic event – the bang of the starting pistol or a collision between racers.

← Write your title here.

Who's in the running?

Who's taking part? Teams representing rival cities or planets? A group of friends? Deadly enemies?

Does one racer try to sabotage another's chances? Do the racers have to overcome any obstacles?

What kind of a race is it? A dragon race? A cycle race through mountains and deserts? A space race?

Is it a contest to see who can build the best vehicle? A race across air, land and sea to the South Pole?

Continue on the next page.

Suspense

Keep readers guessing who will win the race. Perhaps the two lead racers are neck-and-neck most of the way, or one keeps overtaking the other.

Think about the unexpected. Does someone from the back of the race suddenly surge forward and take the lead?

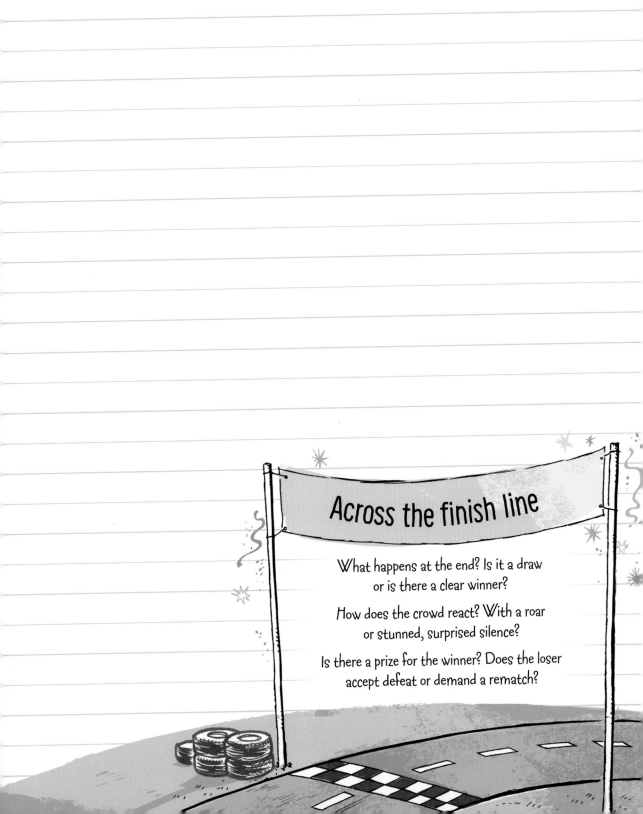

Across the finish line

What happens at the end? Is it a draw
or is there a clear winner?

How does the crowd react? With a roar
or stunned, surprised silence?

Is there a prize for the winner? Does the loser
accept defeat or demand a rematch?

Poetic forms

Many poems use a set pattern of rhymes, rhythms or syllables called a *form*. Writing formal poetry can be like solving a puzzle.

Here are a a couple of poetic forms for you to try out.

The Clerihew

Named after its inventor, Edmund Clerihew Bentley, this form of poem pokes fun at famous people — living or historical.

The poem is made up of four lines, divided into pairs known as couplets.

The first line ends with a famous person's name.

> Fearsome, friendless Genghis Khan
> was never much to look upon.
> But he was taller by a head
> than anyone who comment-ed.

The first two and the last two lines rhyme — although the rhymes can be fairly loose.

....

....

....

....

The haiku

The haiku is a very short poem invented in Japan. Its first line
has five syllables, the second has seven, and the third has five.

① ② ③ ④ ⑤
Cold rain follows mist:

① ② ③ ④⑤ ⑥ ⑦
the monkey also longs for

①②③ ④ ⑤
a little raincoat.

Many haiku include a word or image that refers to a specific season.
Here, "cold rain" suggests it's probably early winter.

Try writing your own haiku.
You could use some of the seasonal words below.

Give your
haiku a
title.

Seasonal words Snowman Bonfire Barefoot

Falling leaves **Heat wave** Straw hat CRICKETS **Hot chocolate**

Mosquito Blossom Harvest Buds Frost

Microfiction

Microfiction, also known as flash fiction, is a way of telling very short stories: usually not more than 100 words long; sometimes as short as five or six.

The 100 word challenge

Try writing a story in exactly 100 words. You could start with a longer story you've already written and then cut it.

Flash fiction tips

- Go through your story and cut non-essential words.
- You don't have space to build characters and set the scene, so get straight to the action.
- Since you have so few words to play with, make the title add something to the story.

The shortest story

It's said that the author Ernest Hemingway was challenged to write a six-word novel, and he came up with this:

"For sale: baby shoes, never worn."

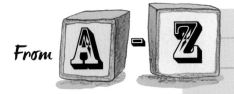

Make it even shorter

Now try writing your own six-word story. You can base it on your 100-word story, or start from scratch.

Borrow from others

Try using elements of familiar stories, such as the sinking of the Titanic, or a fairy tale. This will give your story a context so you don't have to use precious words to explain the setting or characters.

From

Try writing a story in which the first word begins with A, the next word with B, and the next C, until you get to Z.

For example, 'After Ben caught Diana eavesdropping...'

SHOCK JOURNALISM

Journalists use all sorts of techniques to make their readers feel sad, indignant, or enraged. This is known as 'emotive' writing.

Sensational writing

Choosing dramatic and extreme words can help create strong feelings in your reader. Adding extra adjectives and adverbs can help to hammer the point home too.

Dog **left** in forest ⟶ **Helpless** puppy **cruelly abandoned** in forest.

adjective   adverb

Man hit by robber ⟶ **Pensioner attacked by vicious robber.**

Try making these sentences more sensational and emotive.

Ice causes traffic problems.

Woman dies from illness.

Pet dog saves owner.

What makes you angry?

On the next page, write a newspaper article about something that makes you really angry. Try to make the reader feel as angry as you are about it.

Not being allowed ice cream for breakfast?

Cruelty to animals?

Global injustice?

Men getting paid more than women?

Choose a dramatic, attention-grabbing headline, that immediately stirs readers' emotions.

Make them think

Try using rhetorical questions — these are questions asked for effect, that don't have an answer. For example, "How could anyone abandon a puppy?" Questions phrased in this way force your readers to agree with you.

Emotive words

UNJUST Cruel Angered *Horrendous* **Unforgivable**

Dreadful Inhumane Disgusting Outrageous

Read this book

The cover of a book has to call out to readers. Your writing might be brilliant, but no one will find out if they don't pick it up.

Front

Design the front cover for a story you've written, or a book you'd like to write. It could be a book of poems or articles, or a novel.

- Your title should stand out. It could take up the whole page, sit above or below a picture, or could be part of the picture.

- Include your name. It can be your real name, or a made-up pen-name.

- If you have room, add an illustration which gives an impression of what the book's about, and creates a mood that sums it up.

What effect do you want your cover to have?

Shrouded in mystery?   Shocking?   Interesting and intriguing?   Decorative and pretty?   Abstract?

Back

Now write a short summary of your book to go on the back cover. This is known as 'blurb'. It should entice people to open the book and start reading.

You could end your blurb with a cliffhanger to entice your readers. For example:

"Little did he know just how difficult it was going to be..."

"But that was just the beginning..."

"Everything was about to change..."

You could include a price, a barcode, and the name of your publishing company in the corner.

Really sell your story by including quotes from reviewers, or from authors you love.

"Shockingly good!"

"This is writing at its best."

"The most exciting plot of the 21st century"

"A storming tale!"

Keep on writing

The more you write, the better you'll get. Here are some tips to keep you writing.

Fanfiction

Stories based on books, movies and TV shows you've read and watched are known as fanfiction (or fanfic). Fanfic writers use existing characters and settings to create new stories.

Slap it down on the page

Don't worry about whether what you're writing is any good. Most writers write many drafts of each story or piece of writing. The first draft is just there to put something — anything — down on paper. You can worry about making it good later.

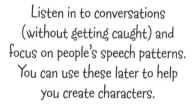

Listen in to conversations (without getting caught) and focus on people's speech patterns. You can use these later to help you create characters.

Take a break

If you're ever stuck while writing, go for a walk or do something else that you find fun. Your ideas might start flowing once you're not trying to write.

Write a letter to your past self. What advice would you give yourself?

Carry a notebook and keep one beside your bed, to jot down ideas whenever they come to you. Inspiration can strike at odd times.

Compete

Enter writing competitions and submit your stories and articles to magazines and websites. You can find some suggestions at the Usborne Quicklinks site.

Entering competitions isn't only about winning — it can also help motivate you to finish a piece of writing.

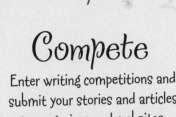

Read more non-fiction. Read more of everything. Reading is like food for your brain. It gives you ideas and helps you decide what type of writing you like best.

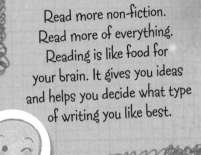

Many brains are better than one

Ask friends and family to read your work or post it online. If people point out problems with it, use that as an opportunity to make your writing better. Professional writers have editors to help them with this.

If you can't make a piece of writing work, try a different approach. For example, turn it into a list, or a rant, or a dialogue, or a poem, or a picture.

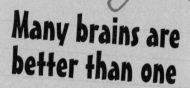

Read your writing out loud. It will help you to spot parts that don't flow well, or don't make sense.

Experiment with all forms of writing. Write plays. Write TV scripts. Write an article explaining something you've learned in science class. Write stories for very young children. Create your own language and use it to write a secret diary entry.

What next?

Use this page to write lists of ideas that you'd like to work on next. What form will each idea take? Will it be a poem, story, article, blog post, novel, play, movie script — or something else?

Idea:

Form:

Idea:

Form:

Idea:

Form:

Idea:

Form:

Idea:

Form:

Books that make you want to write

Keep a list below of books that have inspired you. You could include ones you hated that made you think, "I could do better than this!"

Glossary

Here are some useful writing words that appear in this book.

Adjective: a describing word

Adverb: a word used to describe a verb. For example, "She swam **quickly**."

Alliteration: using repeated consonants (letters that aren't *vowels*) at the start of words. For example, "A pot of pickled peppers."

Assonance: using repeated *vowel* sounds. For example, "Go low in your solo."

Article: a piece of factual writing, often in a newspaper or online.

Blog: short for 'web log', an online journal. Can be about any topic.

Blurb: writing that goes on the back of a book to encourage people to buy it.

Caption: (in comics) used to get across extra information, a little like a *third person narrator*. (in articles) a line used to describe a picture.

Characterization: the way a character is described and brought to life.

Clerihew: a *poetic form* that pokes fun at famous people.

Dialogue: when characters talk in a story or script.

Emotive writing: writing that's designed to create strong feelings in whoever reads it.

Flashback: when a story goes back in time to tell events that happened earlier on.

First person: when a story is told through the eyes of one of the characters.

Genre: a group of stories that share themes, settings and *plot* structures, for example, ghost stories.

Haiku: a *poetic form* from Japan, that uses a set pattern of *syllables* and is usually about nature or the seasons.

Headline: A snappy sentence or phrase at the start of an *article*, designed to make people want to read on.

Imagery: description that conjures up pictures in a reader's mind.

Listicle: an *article* in the form of a list.

Metaphor: describing one thing as another. For example, "The ocean was a roaring monster."

Microfiction: very short stories. Also known as flash fiction.

Muscular writing: using strong *verbs* and short, punchy sentences.

Narrator: the 'voice' telling a story. This can be a character, or someone outside the story.

Plot: the events in a story, and the order in which they appear.

Poetic form: a set pattern of *rhymes*, rhythms and/or *syllables* in a poem.

Poetry: writing in which the words become a kind of music, and how a word sounds is very important.

Point of view: the person through whose eyes a story is seen. (See *narrator*)

Prose: writing that isn't *poetry*.

Rhyme: when two sounds match, often used in *poetry*. A rhyme scheme is a pattern of rhymes in a poem.

Screenplay: the script for a movie or TV show.

Second person: a *narrator* that uses 'you' rather than 'I'. Quite unusual.

Setting: the place where a story takes place.

Simile: comparing one thing to another, usually using the words 'as' or 'like'. For example, "The ocean was roaring like a monster."

Slogan: a short, snappy phrase used in advertments or political campaigns.

Speech bubble: a bubble drawn around speech in a comic strip.

Spoilers: when you give away the *plot* of a story.

Suspense: keeping a reader guessing by witholding information.

Syllable: a single sound in a word. For example, the word 'syllable' has three syllables.

Third person: when a story is told by a *narrator* outside the story.

Thought bubble: like a speech bubble, but cloud-shaped, drawn around the words that represent a character's thoughts in a comic.

Verb: an action or doing word.

Vowels: the letters a, e, i, o and u.

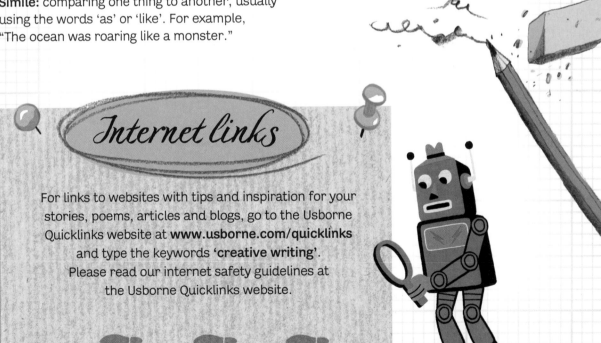

Internet links

For links to websites with tips and inspiration for your stories, poems, articles and blogs, go to the Usborne Quicklinks website at **www.usborne.com/quicklinks** and type the keywords **'creative writing'**. Please read our internet safety guidelines at the Usborne Quicklinks website.

The team behind this book

Illustrators

Lucile Gomez
Paul Hoppe
Briony May Smith
Paul Thurlby

Writing ideas and tips

Louie Stowell
Megan Cullis, Rachel Firth, Rosie Hore, Alice James,
Jerome Martin and Jonathan Melmoth

Designers

Laura Wood and Freya Harrison

Edited by

Ruth Brocklehurst

Acknowledgements

The publishers are grateful to the following for permission to reproduce material: Pages 9, 54, 91 Clipboard, sunstock/Thinkstock; Pages 4, 20 Note paper over white background, robbiverte/Thinkstock; Page 71 Oval frame, WimL/Thinkstock; Page 72 Golden decorative empty picture frame, mkos83/Thinkstock.